The Quant
Enhancing Your Mag. .... a Parallel Life

By Baal Kadmon

Copyright Information

Kadmon, Baal

The Quantum Magician – Enhancing Your Magick with A Parallel Life

–1st ed

Printed in the United States of America

Cover image: 66571244 - Space TIme and Quantum Physics - ⌐ rolffimages

Book Cover Design: Baal Kadmon

Disclaimer

Want to Enhance Your Rituals?

I am not one to promote myself. I like to keep things low-key, but I created a new service that has proven to enhance your rituals and your state of mind, and I am very excited about it. As many of you may know, I use Brainwave Entrainment Audios to enhance my writing, my rituals, and a lot more. I have been using brainwave products since the 80s. I am using one now as I write this.

I have created hyper-specific brainwave audios geared to specific spiritual entities. For example, if you call upon the demon King Paimon, I have a specific audio for him. If you work with the Hindu Goddess Lakshmi, I have a brainwave audio for her as well.

Please visit: www.occultmindscapes.com

I am adding audios every week and will have something for everyone and for every tradition. I am only charging $3.95 per audio MP3 download, with steep discounts for multiple purchases.

1300 have been sold already, I think you will LOVE them.

Introduction

This book is an experiment and you and I are the test subjects. I have used this technique several times and found it quite effective and increasingly more interesting as I delve deeper into it. Now, I am introducing it to you. Nothing like this has been written to date. These concepts have never been melded in such a way before. In this book we will be experimenting with a phenomenon called Quantum Jumping. You have probably heard of this before and yes, some elements of Quantum Jumping will be in this book but that is where the commonalities end. In this book we will be performing Magick but not in the way I have explained in my other books. In this book we will be performing Magick to influence our lives today by performing your ritual in a parallel universe. You will meet your magician doppelgänger whose Magick is always effective and you will meld with him or her. I know this sounds absolutely outlandish and, in many ways,, it is. Despite the oddness of it, it is truly revolutionary. If you do not gain benefit you can always return this book to Amazon. One thing is for certain, you will experience Magick in a brand new way, you will experience Magick on a new level. You will experience Magick like you never have before.

Let us explore your quantum magician.

What Is A Quantum Jump?

If you have been around as long as I have you have probably
come across some very unique modalities of self-help and
Magick. Some are quite practical and easy to understand, that is
the kind of Magick I like to teach and perform. Then there are
modalities and Magickal systems that are so outlandish that it is
often hard to believe they exist, much less that they will be of
any use to the aspiring or advanced magician. One modality
which seems rather outlandish is the concept of Quantum
Jumping. Although Quantum Jumping as a scientific principle is
known, (i.e. how one electron jumps to another position within
an atom). This usage of the term Quantum Jumping is
altogether different.

I was first introduced to Quantum Jumping through the work of
Burt Goldman, an eccentric, grandfatherly teacher who has
some very interesting material. He has a very matter of fact
attitude and is very laidback. Despite his disarming demeanor,
he is quite powerful. He has decades of spiritual knowledge and
practice under him. He worked with the great Guru
Paramahansa Yogananda as well as Jose Silva of the famed
"Silva Method". Since Burt Goldmans' release of the Quantum
Jumping program, others have also added their two cents.
Unfortunately, it appears they have not credited Burt for the

tremendous work he has done bringing this powerful technique to light.

Quantum Jumping is essentially a visualization technique, but here is the difference. Instead of visualizing yourself performing Magick or whatever it is you want to achieve, you tap into alternative versions of yourself that exist in parallel universes. This might sound farfetched, but it is far more effective than traditional visualizations and who is to say you are not truly jumping into another universe in your mind when you do a Quantum Jump? If you look online, you will see that several hundred thousand people have used Quantum Jumping and many of them have achieved their lifelong goals, many have developed talents they previously did not have, all by tapping into an alternative self that already possessed these talents. Do you see how this could be of use to you? I ask that you try the exercises in this book before you pass judgments. If you feel it is not of any use, you may return this book to amazon.com. In the next chapter, I will go over some of the scientific information that exists for the existence of parallel universes.

The concept of the multiverse, or multiple universes has been around for a long time. The concept is very interesting and has implications far beyond anything I could cover in a single book or even a series of books. I will attempt, in this chapter to give you an idea of what the multiverse theory is and its implications for Magick.

As the theory goes, the multiverse concept states that there is an infinite number of universes in which every single permutation of our lives is either taking place or has taken place. Even the minutest details are captured here. For example, you are reading this book and this particular chapter; in an alternative universe every single aspect of your current state is the same but in it, you are several paragraphs ahead. Yes, even such minor differences can simultaneously exist, now multiply these by infinity, and you will see just how mind blowing this is; infinitesimal changes exist eternally. On a grander scale this also means that at one point you were a King or a Queen. Since some multiverse theories posit the existence of infinite possibilities, you were the President of the United States or Prime Minster of Britain. You were Genghis Kahn or Cleopatra. Within the context of the multiverse, all this is possible. Since infinity is removed from time, there is another life right now in which you are those very people I just stated. Some have said that Deja vu experiences are, in fact, experiences of tapping into a parallel universe in which you are experiencing the same event. You simply "clicked" into the parallel for that moment.

There are many names for this theory; some of the more notable ones are "alternate universes, parallel universes, dimensional planes, alternate timelines, alternate realities, parallel worlds, parallel dimensions, and quantum universes" as well as others. Many notable, modern day physicists believe in the possible existence of a multiverse. Some of the more popular being Michio Kaku, Neil deGrasse Tyson, Stephen Hawking and Brian Greene to name a few. Now I must clarify that they may not necessarily agree with the concept of Quantum Jumping as expressed in this book, they still do have many great ideas regarding the existence of a multiverse.

This concept as I stated before is not new, Plato was very much ensconced in the idea and it was the backbone behind Platonism; his discussion of upper and lower realities as just one example. Even in such tales as the 'One thousand and one Arabian Nights' one finds the story "The adventure of Bulukiya" the concept of alternate universes is quite strong, although that is a work of fiction, it is still interesting that such ideas were common place. If we go even further back, we find in the spiritual Hindu texts called the Puranas, they state the existence of an infinite number of universes and that in some of these the typical laws of nature as we know them on earth are different. Magick exists naturally in those universes.

The Great Inflation – How Multiverses come into being

As you may know, the popular theory is that the universe came into existence at the Big Bang. As matter shot out from the singularity it created something called inflation or rapid expansion. To give you an idea of how powerful this explosion was, the singularity which comprised maybe a single nanometer in size, exploded into 250-300 million light years in a trillionth of a second. This amount of energy and speed is nothing we can truly wrap our heads around. Once inflation begins it is generally believed that it will never stop. However, there are regions within the space-time continuum where the inflation does stop and it is in these areas that other universes are formed. Some have called them "bubble universes". Since inflation is infinitely occurring and will never stop, the theory goes that the regions in which it does stop to form other universes is also practically infinite in nature. We may not be able to physically travel to other universes since we have not yet created a vehicle that can travel distances of such magnitude, people have been able to collapse time and space and enter the multiverse in their minds. It is in light of this, you and I are here together, experimenting with Quantum Magick.

The Infinity of Outcomes

In light of this parallel world hypothesis we can now get our heads around the reality of infinite outcomes. As I stated, because of the infinity of outcomes, you have a parallel out there, somewhere, that has all the Magickal abilities you so desire right now. This parallel may exist on a parallel version of our earth or may be on a completely different world altogether. The implications of which is most profound. Although you may have certain limitations on this earth, some real and some perceived, your parallel or doppelganger does not have these limits while some might have more. For our purposes we want to tap into the doppelganger that has what we want. Since the probabilities are infinite, we will focus on the parallel you on earth, since you do want to hone your Magickal powers on earth, don't you? These parallels will have all the knowledge you will need. You can ask him or her for guidance on how to make your Magick work more effectively, you can observe how he or she performs Magick OR, you can meld with this parallel and bring the skills back to your current state. That is my preferred method. Yes, I know this sounds like a fantasy, but I assure you, you will learn something very valuable from your experiments with a parallel life. Are you truly jumping into another universe? Maybe, maybe not, it could all be taking place in the subconscious mind. This is fine because the subconscious mind does, in fact, have everything you need to make your Magick more effective. Even if it does turn out to be the subconscious mind, that is fine. You see, the subconscious mind, as you experience it has certain limitations that you have placed on yourself instilled within it. Whenever you try to do something counter to your subconscious mind, you end up thwarted because what you are trying to do is running counter to your day-to-day experience. If you are sabotaging yourself, that is the subconscious at work. Have you ever tried to change a habit? You realize it is hard because your subconscious mind does not want to relinquish the power of that habit. However, with Quantum Jumping, the subconscious mind is being presented with an alternative image of yourself. It is being tricked into believing you are actually looking at someone else. So, when you see your idealized self you can easily learn from it since the subconscious mind is no longer fighting you. I know this is a bit complicated, but that is what is happening. Now, of course, it may very well be a multiverse experiencing you are having. In either case, I wanted to also illustrate that it doesn't really matter if it is a multiverse or just your subconscious mind being unlocked in a way that leads to the least resistance. In my personal experience, I have used this method about a dozen times. I have asked for guidance on various matters, not just on Magick. One that stands out for me is where I live. I tapped into my multiverse parallel that had the apartment that I wanted. It was the same one I am in now, but redone. This experiment started earlier this year. I did this ritual twice. Within 6 months I not only redid my apartment, the funds that were required materialized and is still materializing. I know you may not believe me, but it is the truth nonetheless. I ask you give this method a try. Now, you can use this method for whatever it is you like. We will be performing rituals in this Multiverse state that will deal with certain specific desires. We will cover those shortly. The only limit you can place on this is your own. If outcomes are infinite, so can your results be.

So Mote it be.

Your First Quantum Jump

We will now perform a quick experiment. I will guide you through your first Quantum Jump. In this one, I want you to think of an issue that you would like some clarity on. (We will do the rituals a bit later). It can be any issue you have. Our intention here is to find the parallel you who has resolved it. Mind you, the parallel may take on a form you are not familiar with. Since the outcomes are infinite, you may be of the opposite sex during your Quantum Jump. That is okay, you will know it is you. Pay close attention to what it tells you, it may be in words or it may be in a feeling or glimpses. The insight you glean will help you understand the issue you are currently having. You may meld into the parallel you or you may take its advice. Let us now do a Quantum Jump.

Here are the steps:

This step is optional, but I like to say a prayer to my patron goddesses before I do a Quantum Jump. I do this to ensure that whatever it is I see and learn will be for my highest good. My patrons tend to be the Goddess Tara, Kali, Durga, Isis and the Mother Mary.

Find a place where you will not be disturbed for 15-30 minutes.

You can play relaxing music, light incense and or candles if it will help you relax.

Think of the issue you are having.

State the intention that you wish to meet your parallel who has resolved this issue.

Sit with your eyes closed and breathe deeply.

Once relaxed, picture yourself walking through a hallway with many doors, each door represents one of your parallel lives.

Pick the door you are most drawn to and open it.

Step into the room, it may transform into another scene, the most important thing is to step through the door.

Find your parallel and greet it. Ask it whatever you want.

When you are satisfied you can slowly open your eyes and return to normal. You can thank it if you like. (What I do is imagine myself meld with the parallel and then come back here)

You will notice that your hair on your arms and body will stand on end, this is normal; you have literally tapped into another you. I highly recommend you keep a pen and paper handy or a recorder, so you can record the insight you have gleaned.

As you can see, this is quite simple. Try it a few times and you will notice that you will gain knowledge you did not initially have. I promise you that, no matter what, it will be an interesting trip.

If you have read my other books you know that I use very few props in my rituals. The instruments I do use are basic and optional. You do not need to have any of these items. I personally like using them because they ground and anchor my mind for the ritual but are by no means necessary for this to work.

Here is a list of things that will help you with your rituals.

Frankincense and Myrrh: This Incense is a wonderful sacred fragrance and was once more precious than gold. It was so valuable that people would rather it, than gold itself.

Red Chime Candles: This color is quite powerful for love rituals and rituals of power.

Gold Candles: This candle will be used for the ritual on financial assistance. Many occultists will tell you to use green, but this has been a long-held misconception. The only reason why people have said to use green is because it's the color of money. The thing is, it's only the color of money in the U.S.A and maybe a few notes here and there of other nations. They don't call the dollar the "greenback" for nothing. Green is not a color that is truly indicative money. Gold is though, Gold is UNIVERSALLY known to be a signifier of wealth both in ancient times and present. If you have been using green for your money rituals, now you know to use gold instead. It is much more effective.

White Candles: White is for purity.

Silver candles: This is the color of wisdom as well as for Magickal powers.

Blue Candles: This will be used for health.

Black Candles: These candles will be used to conquer your enemies and repel evil spiritual entities.

Notebook: To write down any messages you might receive.

(Optional) A Sony Digital Flash Recorder (or other digital recorder) if you rather dictate the messages and insights.

As you can see, there is no need for anything elaborate. In the next chapter, I will take you through seven Quantum Jumps.

They will be on:

1. To Gain Protection

2. To gain Wisdom and Intuition

3. To conquer ones enemies

4. To promote Physical Healing

5. To gain Prosperity.

6. To find ones purpose

7. To gain talents and abilities.

Now we will go through seven rituals, but first I will go through the steps. I will repeat the steps for every ritual as well for easy reference.

Here are the steps:

This step is optional, but I like to say a prayer to my patron goddesses before I do a Quantum jump. I do this to ensure that whatever it is I see and learn will be for my highest good. My patrons tend to be the Goddess Tara, Kali, Durga, Isis and the mother Mary.

Find a place where you will not be disturbed for 15-30 minutes.

Light incense and or candles if it will help you relax.

Think of the issue you are having.

State the intention that you wish to meet your parallel who has resolved this issue.

Sit with your eyes closed and breathe deeply.

Once relaxed, picture yourself walking through a hallway with many doors, each door represents one of your parallel lives.

Pick the door you are most drawn to and open it.

Step into the room, it may transform into another scene, the most important thing is to step through the door.

Find your parallel and greet it. Ask it whatever you want.

Make sure you have a pen or the recorder handy to record your results.

When you are satisfied you can slowly open your eyes and return to normal waking consciousness. You can thank it if you like. (What I do is imagine myself meld with the parallel and then come back here).

Quantum Magician Ritual – 1: To Gain Protection

Say a prayer of intention if you like.

Light the incense and a blue and a black candle.

Think of the issue you are having. Do you want to master protection Magick?

State the intention that you wish to meet your parallel who has this power.

Sit with your eyes closed and breathe deeply.

Once relaxed, picture yourself walking through a hallway with many doors, each door represents one of your parallel lives.

Pick the door you are most drawn to and open it.

Step into the room, it may transform into another scene, the most important thing is to step through the door.

Find your parallel and greet it. Ask it what it is you need. What does he or she look like? How can they help you with your need for protection? Is it telling you a method? Or do you see it perform a protection ritual?

Make sure you have a pen or the recorder handy to record your results.

Now slowly meld with this parallel you and feel his or her power enter your body and mind. Now open your eyes. You now have the information and power to perform protection rituals that truly work.

Quantum Magician Ritual – 2: To Gain Wisdom and Intuition

Say a prayer of intention if you like.

Light the incense and the white and silver candles.

Think of the issue you are having. Why do you want to gain wisdom and or intuition?

State the intention that you wish to meet your parallel who has this trait.

Sit with your eyes closed and breathe deeply.

Once relaxed, picture yourself walking through a hallway with many doors, each door represents one of your parallel lives.

Pick the door you are most drawn to and open it.

Step into the room, it may transform into another scene, the most important thing is to step through the door.

Find your parallel and greet it. Ask it what it is you need. What does he or she look like? How can they help you with your development and acquisition of knowledge and intuition? Is it telling you a method? Or do you see it perform a ritual?

Make sure you have a pen or the recorder handy to record your results.

Now slowly meld with this parallel you and feel his or her power enter your body and mind. Now open your eyes. You now have the information and intuitive powers to gain wisdom.

Quantum Magician Ritual – 3: To Conquer Ones Enemies

Say a prayer of intention if you like.

Light the incense and the white and black candles.

Think of the issue you are having. Who is it that you want to control and conquer?

State the intention that you wish to meet your parallel who has what you need.

Sit with your eyes closed and breathe deeply.

Once relaxed, picture yourself walking through a hallway with many doors, each door represents one of your parallel lives.

Pick the door you are most drawn to and open it.

Step into the room, it may transform into another scene, the most important thing is to step through the door.

Find your parallel and greet it. Ask it what it is you need. What does he or she look like? How does your parallel conquer his or her enemies with Magick? Is it telling you a method? Or do you see it perform a ritual?

Make sure you have a pen or the recorder handy to record your results.

Now slowly meld with this parallel you and feel his or her power enter your body and mind. Now open your eyes. You now have the information and abilities to control and conquer your enemies.

Say a prayer of intention if you like.

Light the incense and a blue candle.

Think of the issue you are having. Where do you need healing most?

State the intention that you wish to meet your parallel who has this healed in them.

Sit with your eyes closed and breathe deeply.

Once relaxed, picture yourself walking through a hallway with many doors, each door represents one of your parallel lives.

Pick the door you are most drawn to and open it.

Step into the room, it may transform into another scene, the most important thing is to step through the door.

Find your parallel and greet it. Ask it what it is you need. What does he or she look like? Does it have a cure for your ailment? How does he or she manage it?

Make sure you have a pen or the recorder handy to record your results.

Now slowly meld with this parallel you and feel his or her power enter your body and mind. Now open your eyes. You now have the information and abilities to heal yourself and others.

Say a prayer of intention if you like.

Light the incense and the gold and silver candles.

Think of the issue you are having. Do you owe money? Or do you want general prosperity?

State the intention that you wish to meet your parallel who is already wealthy.

Sit with your eyes closed and breathe deeply.

Once relaxed, picture yourself walking through a hallway with many doors, each door represents one of your parallel lives.

Pick the door you are most drawn to and open it.

Step into the room, it may transform into another scene, the most important thing is to step through the door.

Find your parallel and greet it. Ask it what it is you need. What does he or she look like? Is he or she wealthy? Ask it how it became wealthy? Does what he or she say resonate with you?

Make sure you have a pen or the recorder handy to record your results.

Now slowly meld with this parallel you and feel his or her power enter your body and mind. Now open your eyes. You now have the information and abilities to gain prosperity.

Say a prayer of intention if you like.

Light the incense and the white candle.

Think of the issue you are having. Are you feeling aimless in your life? Do you feel that you have no direction in life?

State the intention that you wish to meet your parallel who has found their life purpose.

Sit with your eyes closed and breathe deeply.

Once relaxed, picture yourself walking through a hallway with many doors, each door represents one of your parallel lives.

Pick the door you are most drawn to and open it.

Step into the room, it may transform into another scene, the most important thing is to step through the door.

Find your parallel and greet it. Ask it what it is you need. What does he or she look like? Is he or she fulfilled in life? Ask it how it became that way? Does what he or she say resonate with you?

Make sure you have a pen or the recorder handy to record your results.

Now slowly meld with this parallel you and feel his or her power enter your body and mind. Now open your eyes. You will now be open to insights as to what you should do in your life.

Quantum Magician Ritual – 7: To Gain Talents and Abilities

Say a prayer of intention if you like.

Light the incense and the white and gold candles.

Think of the issue you are having. What is it that you want to master and gain abilities to or for?

State the intention that you wish to meet your parallel who has the talents and abilities that you want.

Sit with your eyes closed and breathe deeply.

Once relaxed, picture yourself walking through a hallway with many doors, each door represents one of your parallel lives.

Pick the door you are most drawn to and open it.

Step into the room, it may transform into another scene, the most important thing is to step through the door.

Find your parallel and greet it. Ask it what it is you need. What does he or she look like? Does he or she have these talents and abilities? Ask it how it attained them. Does what he or she say resonate with you?

Make sure you have a pen or the recorder handy to record your results.

Now slowly meld with this parallel you and feel his or her power enter your body and mind. Now open your eyes. You will now be open to insights as to how to gain those abilities. You might find yourself suddenly getting really good very fast at the chosen skill or ability. This is not uncommon.

Conclusion

This concludes The Quantum Magician. As you have seen, it is quite simple. You can do these rituals as often as you like. You can also do multiple Quantum Jumps for the same issue and see what information you can glean. As you see, there is no pomp and circumstance, no expensive ritual garments and paraphernalia, no odd and impossible herbs to obtain, no directions to turn to, no contrived and pompous terminology and phrases to this kind of Magick. Just Magick , unconventional Magick at that. I am filled with utmost confidence that once you have performed one or all these rituals, you will enter a Magickal partnership with your Quantum – parallel self / selves. I am also convinced that after you use Quantum Jumping in your rituals, you will want to incorporate it into your Magickal repertoire.

And So It Is.

Occult Courses

Over the years, I have received many hundreds of emails asking me if I would ever consider creating online video courses. At first, I was unsure. After so many emails, I decided it was time.

I am now offering courses.

If it interests you in learning more about the **Occult, Meditation, Ancient Languages and History**, you will not be disappointed.

All courses will all be accessible, informative and <u>affordable.</u>

Please go to www.occultcourses.com

There you will find my current courses and all the upcoming courses. If you see a current course you are interested in, you can sign up and get **instant access.**

If you see a future course that interests you, sign up to the mailing list and I will notify you upon its release.

All courses come with a **30-day, no questions asked, money-back guarantee**. If a course is not for you, just let me know, and I will refund you.

Please go to www.occultcourses.com

Want to Enhance Your Rituals?

I am not one to promote myself. I like to keep things low-key, but I created a new service that has proven to enhance your rituals and your state of mind, and I am very excited about it. As many of you may know, I use Brainwave Entrainment Audios to enhance my writing, my rituals, and a lot more. I have been using brainwave products since the 80s. I am using one now as I write this.

I have created hyper-specific brainwave audios geared to specific spiritual entities. For example, if you call upon the demon King Paimon, I have a specific audio for him. If you work with the Hindu Goddess Lakshmi, I have a brainwave audio for her as well.

Please visit: www.occultmindscapes.com

I am adding audios every week and will have something for everyone and for every tradition. I am only charging $3.95 per audio MP3 download, with steep discounts for multiple purchases.

1300 have been sold already, I think you will LOVE them.

Other Books By The Author

Organized by date of publication from most recent:

Surya Mantra Magick (Mantra Magick Series Book 13)

Tiamat Unveiled (Mesopotamian Magick Book 3)

Pazuzu Rising (Mesopotamian Magick Book 2)

BAAL: THE LORD OF THE HEAVENS: CALLING DOWN THE GREAT GOD OF CANAAN (CANAANITE MAGICK Book 2)

Chod Practice Demystified: Severing the Ties That Bind (Baal on Buddhism Book 2)

The Talmud: An Occultist Introduction

The Path of the Pendulum: An Unconventional Approach

Durga Mantra Magick: Harnessing The Power of the Divine Protectress

Asherah: The Queen of Heaven (Canaanite Magick Book 1)

Dependent Origination for the Layman (Baal on Buddhism Book 1)

The Watchers And Their Ways

Rabbi Isaac Luria: The Lion of the Kabbalah (Jewish Mystics Book 1)

Circe's Wand: Empowerment, Enchantment, Magick

Ganesha Mantra Magick: Calling Upon the God of New Beginnings

Shiva Mantra Magick: Harnessing The Primordial

Tefillin Magick: Using Tefillin For Magickal Purposes (Jewish Magick Book 1)

Jesus Magick (Bible Magick Book 2)

The Magickal Moment Of Now: The Inner Mind of the Advanced Magician

The Magick Of Lilith: Calling Upon The Great Goddess of The Left Hand Path (Mesopotamian Magick Book 1)

The Magickal Talismans of King Solomon

Mahavidya Mantra Magick: Tap Into the 10 Goddesses of Power

Jinn Magick: How to Bind the Jinn to do Your Bidding

Magick And The Bible: Is Magick Compatible With The Bible? (Bible Magick Book 1)

The Magickal Rites of Prosperity: Using Different Methods To Magickally Manifest Wealth

Lakshmi Mantra Magick: Tap Into The Goddess Lakshmi for Wealth and Abundance In All Areas of Life

Tarot Magick: Harness the Magickal Power of the Tarot

The Quantum Magician: Enhancing Your Magick With A Parallel Life

Tibetan Mantra Magick: Tap Into The Power Of Tibetan Mantras

The 42 Letter Name of God: The Mystical Name Of Manifestation (Sacred Names Book 6)

Tara Mantra Magick: How To Use The Power Of The Goddess Tara

Vedic Magick: Using Ancient Vedic Spells To Attain Wealth

The Daemonic Companion: Creating Daemonic Entities To Do Your Will

Tap Into The Power Of The Chant: Attaining Supernatural Abilities Using Mantras (Supernatural Attainments Series

72 Demons Of The Name: Calling Upon The Great Demons Of The Name (Sacred Names Book 5)

Moldavite Magick: Tap Into The Stone Of Transformation Using Mantras (Crystal Mantra Magick Book 1)

Ouija Board Magick - Archangels Edition: Communicate And Harness The Power Of The Great Archangels

Chakra Mantra Magick: Tap Into The Magick Of Your Chakras (Mantra Magick Series Book 4)

Seed Mantra Magick: Master The Primordial Sounds Of The Universe (Mantra Magick Series Book 3)

The Magick Of Saint Expedite: Tap Into The Truly Miraculous Power Of Saint Expedite (Magick Of The Saints Book 2)

Kali Mantra Magick: Summoning The Dark Powers of Kali Ma (Mantra Magick Series Book 2)

Mary Magick: Calling Forth The Divine Mother For Help (Magick Of The Saints Book 1)

Vashikaran Magick: Learn The Dark Mantras Of Subjugation (Mantra Magick Series Book 1)

The Hidden Names Of Genesis: Tap Into The Hidden Power Of Manifestation (Sacred Names Book 4)

The 99 Names Of Allah: Acquiring the 99 Divine Qualities of God (Sacred Names Book 3)

The 72 Angels Of The Name: Calling On the 72 Angels of God (Sacred Names)

The 72 Names of God: The 72 Keys To Transformation (Sacred Names Book 1)

About Baal Kadmon

Baal Kadmon is an Author, and Occultist based out of New York City. In addition to the Occult, he is a Religious Scholar, Philosopher and a Historian specializing in Ancient History, Late Antiquity and Medieval History. He has studied and speaks Israeli Hebrew · Classical Hebrew · Ugaritic language · Arabic · Judeo-Aramaic · Syriac (language) · Ancient Greek and Classical Latin.

Baal first discovered his occult calling when he was very young. It was only in his teens, when on a trip to the Middle East that he heeded the call. Several teachers and many decades later he felt ready to share what he has learned.

His teachings are unconventional to say the least. He includes in-depth history in almost all the books he writes, in addition to rituals. He shatters the beloved and idolatrously held notions most occultists hold dear. His pared-down approach to Magick is refreshing and is very much needed in a field that is mired by self-important magicians who place more importance on pomp and circumstance rather than on Magick. What you learn from Baal is straight forward, with no frills. Magick is about bringing about change or a desired result; Magick is a natural birthright...There is no need to complicate it.

Follow Him on Facebook and other Social Media Sites:

http://baalkadmon.com/social-media/

29731339R00028